Making Noise!

Making Sounds

Louise and Richard Spilsbury

Raintree is an imprint of Capstone Global Library Limited,
a company incorporated in England and Wales having its
registered office at 7 Pilgrim Street, London, EC4V 6LB –
Registered company number: 6695582

www.raintreepublishers.co.uk
myorders@raintreepublishers.co.uk
Text © Capstone Global Library Limited 2014
First published in hardback in 2014
The moral rights of the proprietor have been asserted.

Edited by Adam Miller, Sian Smith, and Penny West
Designed by Cynthia Akiyoshi
Original illustrations © Capstone Global Library Ltd 2013
Illustrated by HL Studios
Picture research by Elizabeth Alexander
Originated by Capstone Global Library Ltd
Production by Victoria Fitzgerald
Printed and bound in China by Leo Paper Products Ltd

ISBN 978 1 406 27447 9
17 16 15 14 13
10 9 8 7 6 5 4 3 2 1

Spilsbury, Louise and Richard
Making Noise: Making Sounds (Exploring Sound)
A full catalogue record for this book is available from the British
Library.

Acknowledgements
We would like to thank the following for permission to
reproduce photographs: Alamy pp. 7 (© David Gee 4), 11
(© Emilio Ereza), 15 (© Robert Harding Picture Library Ltd), 19
(© Travel Pictures); Capstone Publishers (© Karon Dubke) pp. 8,
9, 12, 13, 13, 16, 17, 17, 20, 20, 21, 24, 25, 25, 29; Getty Images
pp. 10 (Daniel Boczarski/Redferns), 27 (Nigel Pavitt/
AWL Images); naturepl.com p. 28 (© Nature Production);
Shutterstock pp. 5 (©CCat82), 14 (©Iancu Cristian), 22
(© Mircea Simu); SuperStock p. 4 (Stock Connection); Design
features: Shutterstock © Vass Zoltan, © agsandrew, © Dennis
Tokarzewski, © Mikhail Bakunovich, © ALMAGAMI, © DVARG,
© luckypic.

Cover photograph reproduced with permission of Corbis
(© David Deas/DK Stock).

We would like to thank Ann Fullick for her invaluable help in the
preparation of this book.

Every effort has been made to contact copyright holders of
material reproduced in this book. Any omissions will be rectified
in subsequent printings if notice is given to the publishers.

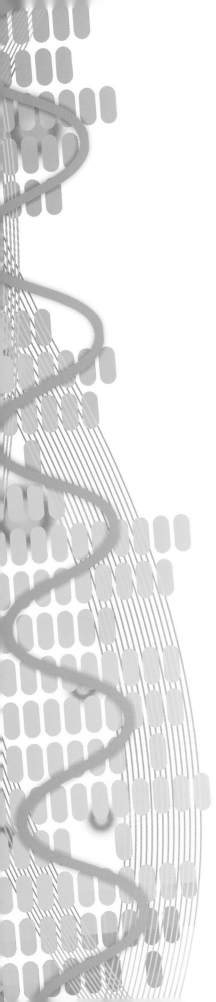

Contents

Some words are shown in **bold**, like this. You can find out what they mean by looking in the glossary.

What makes sounds?

We live in a world full of sounds. Close your eyes for a minute and listen to the sounds around you. What sounds can you hear? Can you tell what is making those sounds? Different things make different sounds. Cats mew, dogs bark, and birds tweet. People sing, shout, whisper, and speak. Cars rumble and honk, and doorbells ring or buzz.

Cities are full of noises made by people, such as cars honking and people talking.

Some sounds happen naturally – for example, the sound of leaves rustling in the trees when the wind blows against them. Some sounds are made by people, such as the sounds of traffic moving on the street or a football being kicked into the air. There are many different sounds, but they are all made when things move in a certain way.

Water splashing is a natural sound.

Vibrations

When things **vibrate**, they make sounds. **Vibrations** happen when an object moves up and down or backwards and forwards very quickly. When we pluck a guitar string or hit a bell, we can see the string and the bell vibrate. Some things make sound vibrations that are too fast to see. If you tap a cup with a spoon, the cup vibrates and makes a sound, even though you cannot see those vibrations.

Stretch a rubber band over an empty shoe box and twang it so it vibrates and makes a sound. When you stop the rubber band vibrating, the sound stops too.

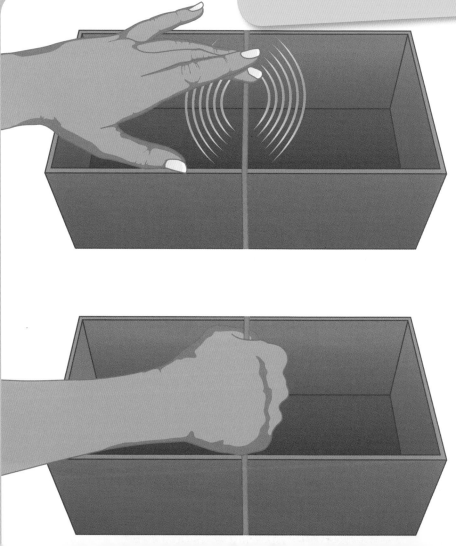

When an object vibrates, it makes the air around it vibrate too. When the air around the object vibrates, it makes the air next to it vibrate. When vibrations travel through the air like this, we call them **sound waves**. When sound waves reach our ears, they make parts inside our ears vibrate so we can hear the sounds.

Can you feel sounds?

Some moving objects make big vibrations that we can feel as well as hear. When a noisy plane passes over a street, it can cause air vibrations that make windows in the houses vibrate and rattle too!

Activity: Feeling vibrations

We cannot see the **vibrations** that make most sounds. Try this activity to prove they are there!

What to do

1 Blow up the balloon very big, but be careful not to pop it. Tie the end tightly so no air gets out.

2 Hold the balloon against your ear.

3 Ask your friend to press their lips against the balloon and speak. What happens?

4

4 Repeat steps 2 and 3, but this time you should speak and your friend should listen.

Try this!

Blow up another balloon, but do not tie it up. Instead, let the air out of it slowly. You should see the opening of the balloon vibrate and make a noise as it does so!

What happens?

When you hold the balloon to your ear, you can hear sound vibrations through the balloon and you can feel them. When you speak into the balloon, you can also feel the sounds you are making as the balloon's skin **vibrates** against your lips. This shows that things make sounds when they move and vibrate the air around them.

Hitting, rattling, and shaking!

All musical instruments use **vibrations** to make sound. **Percussion** instruments **vibrate** and make sounds when we tap or hit them. We hit cymbals against each other, or with sticks, **mallets**, or brushes. Hitting the cymbals in different ways makes them vibrate in different ways so they make different sounds. We shake maracas to make the seeds inside move around and hit the sides. The sides vibrate to make a rattling sound.

When you hit the top of a drum with drumsticks, mallets, or brushes, the skin of the drum vibrates and makes sounds.

Percussion instruments make different sounds depending on the **material** that vibrates. A xylophone has wooden bars you hit with a mallet. They vibrate and make the metal tubes attached to them vibrate too. The vibrating metal tubes make a bell-like sound. Castanets are Spanish instruments made from pieces of wood. They make a clickety-clack sound when you hit them together.

Long ago, people used rain sticks to try to bring on a rainstorm.

Rain sticks

In Chile, people used to make rain sticks from **hollow** cactus plant stems with cactus spikes hammered into them. When they turned the stick upside down, tiny pebbles sealed inside fell to the other end and made a sound like rain. Rain sticks can be used as percussion instruments.

Activity: Make a rain stick

Make your own rain stick.

What to do

What you need
- Poster tube with a lid
- Screws or nails
- Handful of dry lentils, beans, rice, or tiny pasta
- Paper
- Scissors
- Sticky tape
- Pens, crayons, stickers etc to decorate the tube

1 Draw two spiral shapes around the tube so they cross over. Ask an adult to help you put about 40 screws or nails into the side of the tube along the lines, evenly spread out.

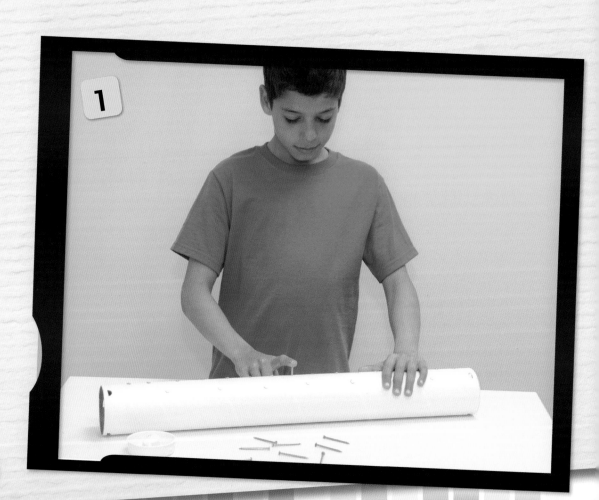

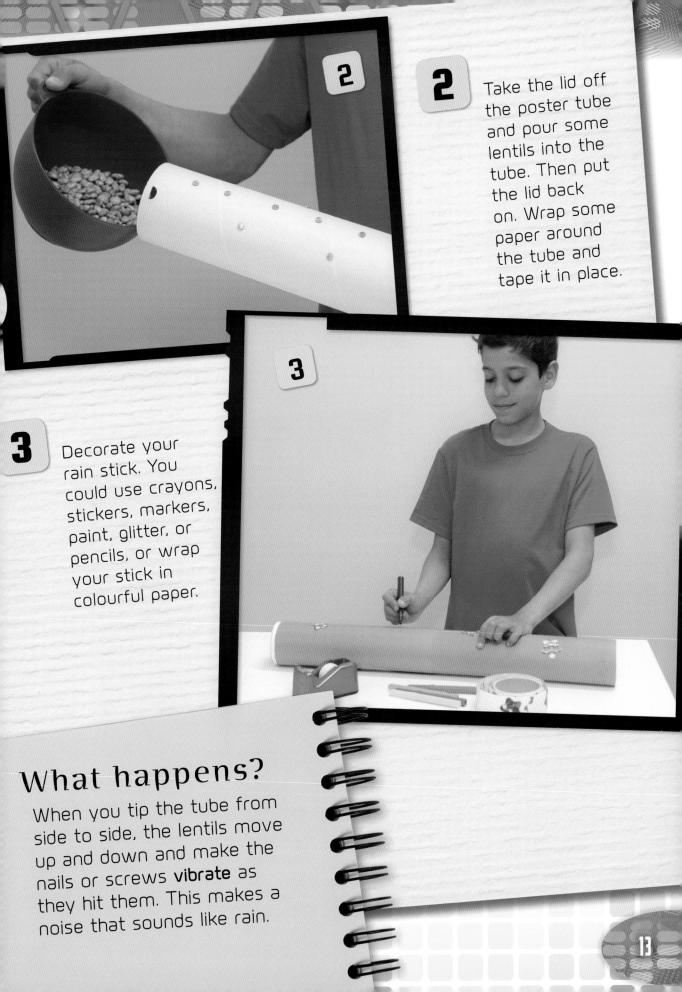

2 Take the lid off the poster tube and pour some lentils into the tube. Then put the lid back on. Wrap some paper around the tube and tape it in place.

3 Decorate your rain stick. You could use crayons, stickers, markers, paint, glitter, or pencils, or wrap your stick in colourful paper.

What happens?

When you tip the tube from side to side, the lentils move up and down and make the nails or screws **vibrate** as they hit them. This makes a noise that sounds like rain.

Playing with strings

String instruments make sounds when their strings **vibrate**. People make the strings vibrate by plucking or strumming them with their fingers or running a bow across them. When we drag a violin bow across a violin string, it pulls on the string a little and makes it vibrate. When we pull on a guitar string with our fingers or a tool called a **pick**, it vibrates too.

Guitars only make musical sounds when we make their strings vibrate.

There are many different types of string instrument. A double bass is like a violin, but when it is standing up on its end it is as tall as a man! As you drag a bow made of horsehair across its strings, the bow sticks and then slips repeatedly to create a **vibration**. The piano is a string instrument too. When we press the keys on a piano, soft hammers hit strings inside the piano. When the hammers hit the strings, the strings vibrate to play notes.

The sitar is a string instrument used mainly in Indian music.

A windy harp?

The aeolian harp is an unusual string instrument. People don't play it, the wind does! Its strings are stretched over an open box and make sounds when the wind blows and vibrates them.

Activity: Make a violin

You can make your own string instrument to see how **vibrating** strings make sounds.

What you need

- Wire clothes hanger
- Nylon string
- Scissors

What to do

1 To make the bow, cut a piece of nylon string about 60 centimetres (24 inches) long. Bend the bottom of the hanger up slightly to create a bow shape. Tie the string to one end of the hanger. Ask someone to hold the string tight while you tie the other end so that it stays tight.

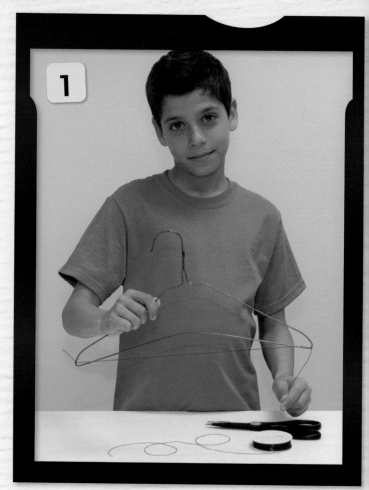

2 Use your fingers to pluck this string and see what sounds you can make.

3 Cut a piece of nylon string about 1 metre (3 feet) long. Tie both ends of it to solid things (such as two table legs) so it is fairly tight.

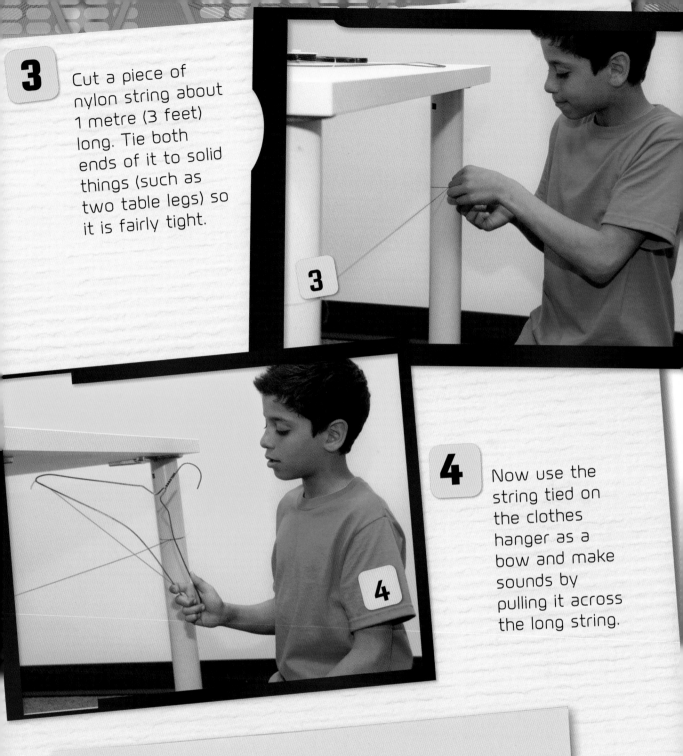

3

4

4 Now use the string tied on the clothes hanger as a bow and make sounds by pulling it across the long string.

What happens?

When you make the strings vibrate, you create sounds. The strings vibrate in different ways. They make different sounds when you pluck them or pull the bow across them.

Tuneful tubes

Wind instruments make sound when the air inside them **vibrates**. Recorders, trumpets, and most other wind instruments have tubes you blow into. Flutes make sounds when you blow air across a **mouthpiece**. The air that goes inside the flute vibrates to make sound, like when you blow across the edge of a bottle. When you blow into clarinets and saxophones, the air travels across a thin piece of wood called a **reed**. The reed vibrates quickly and makes the air inside vibrate too.

When you blow across the mouthpiece of a flute, some of the air goes inside the hollow pipe and vibrates to make sounds.

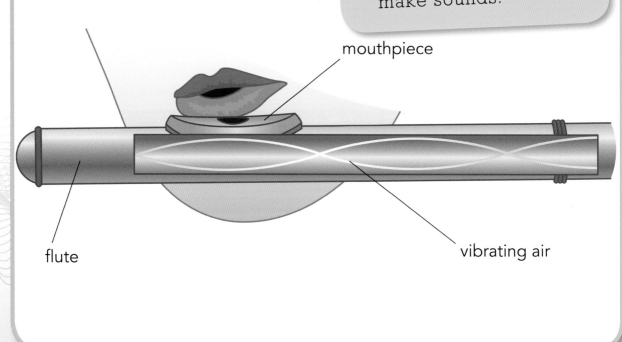

mouthpiece

flute

vibrating air

Every country in the world has wind instruments. The Peruvian ocarina is usually made from clay. It is shaped like a large egg with a hole to blow into at one end and holes over the top. It sounds like a flute. Nose flutes from Hawaii, the Philippines, and New Zealand are made from **hollow** bamboo plant stems. You use your nose to blow air into them!

Didgeridoo

The didgeridoo was first made and played by people in Australia over 1,500 years ago. It is made from a hollow tree branch about 1.5 metres (5 feet) long. Didgeridoos make a sound as your lips vibrate when blowing into the instrument.

Activity: Make a trumpet

Make your own trumpet and experiment with making sounds through tubes.

What to do

1 Ask an adult to cut off the spout of the bottle with a knife. The diameter of the bottle should be slightly bigger than the diameter of the tube. (The diameter is the width of a circle from one side to the other.) The spout of the bottle is your **mouthpiece**.

2 Tape the mouthpiece over one end of the tube.

3 Draw around the plate and cut out the circle of paper. Fold this in half, then in half again. Press it down to make fold lines. Open it out and cut out one quarter of the circle. Then curl the rest up into a cone and use a piece of tape to hold the cone together.

4 Cut off the pointy end of your cone to make a bigger hole to fit over the open end of your tube. Tape it in place.

5 Practise making your lips buzz, as if you are making a sound like a horse! Press your lips onto the mouthpiece and buzz to play your trumpet!

5

What happens?

The buzzing sound a trumpet player makes into their mouthpiece produces sound **vibrations**. Try making your lips buzz faster and slower until you get the best sound from the trumpet.

How your voice works

Your voice is a kind of wind instrument too! Hum with your mouth closed and put your hand on your throat. Can you feel a **vibration**? Air **vibrates** in your throat to make sounds. This is like the way air vibrates inside a wind instrument to make sounds.

Different voices

Why does your voice sound different in a recording? When we speak, vibrations in our throat make bones in our head vibrate too. These vibrations mix with the **sound waves** going into our ears. When you hear a recorded voice, you only sense the vibrations in your ears.

We make sounds when air passes through our throat and makes parts called **vocal cords** vibrate.

How vocal cords make sound

1 Air goes into and out of your **lungs** through a tube in the neck and chest called the **trachea**. At the top of your trachea is your voicebox, or **larynx**.

2 Vocal cords are like **membranes** stretched across the larynx. When you breathe in and out quietly, the vocal cords are relaxed and open, so the air passes them without making sound.

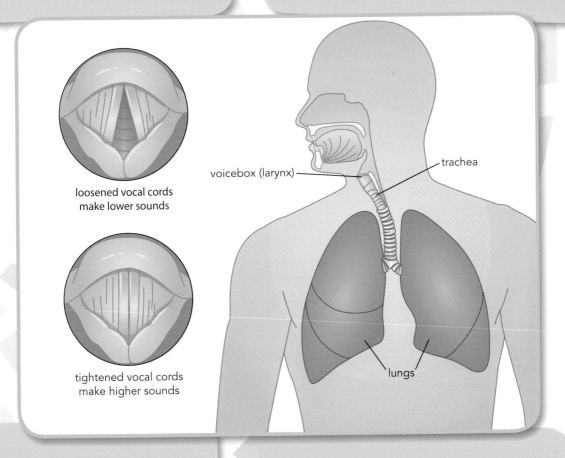

loosened vocal cords
make lower sounds

tightened vocal cords
make higher sounds

voicebox (larynx)

trachea

lungs

3 When you want to make a sound, your vocal cords close across your throat. When the air you breathe out pushes past them, the vocal cords vibrate.

4 When vocal cords vibrate, they make the air vibrate, forming a sound.

5 These vibrations go out of your mouth as sound waves that other people can hear.

Activity: Make a balloon flute

Some wind instruments work like **vocal cords** and **vibrate** a **membrane** to make sounds. This balloon flute is one!

What you need

- Two balloons
- Scissors
- Two elastic bands
- Cardboard tube

What to do

1 Ask an adult to use the scissors to help you make a hole about 1 centimetre (⅓ inch) wide halfway down one side of the tube. Trim off the cardboard carefully to make the edge of the hole smooth and neat.

2 Cut the ends off the two balloons. Stretch one balloon over one end of the tube. Twist on an elastic band to hold it in place.

3 Fix the other balloon over the other end of the tube in the same way. Make sure the balloons are stretched on tightly.

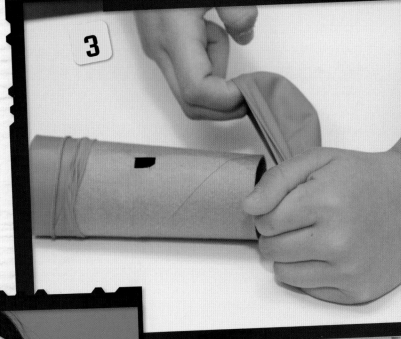

3

4

4 Now, put your lips up to the hole and blow across it gently. You might not get a sound right away, so keep trying!

What happens?

The membranes at the ends of the instrument vibrate when you blow air across the hole on the tube and make sounds. This is a bit like the way the vocal cords vibrate when air from the **lungs** blows on them.

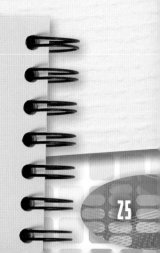

Sound and language

We make different sounds in our throat so we can say different words, whisper, sing, or shout. **Muscles** in the **larynx** stretch and loosen the **vocal cords** when air from your **lungs** passes over them. This changes the way the vocal cords **vibrate**, so they make high sounds and low sounds. To make specific sounds and words, we move our tongue, lips, and teeth to change how the air comes out.

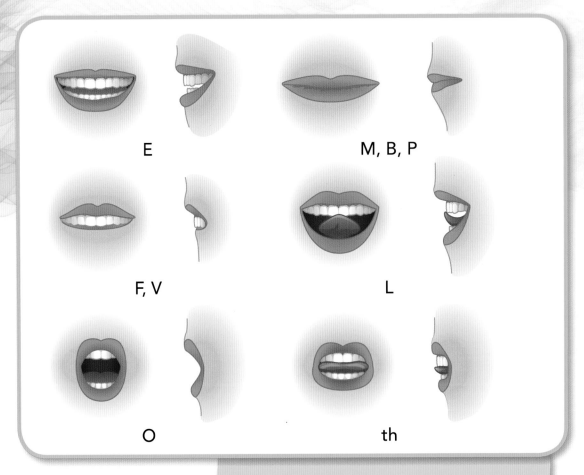

E

M, B, P

F, V

L

O

th

This is how we change the shape of our mouths to help us make some different sounds.

Words that click

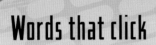

The Khoisan languages of Southern Africa use many different clicking and tutting sounds to make words. These languages may have started among hunters who used words that sounded like insect calls so the animals they hunted did not hear them.

Different languages use different speech sounds. That is why someone speaking a foreign language makes slightly different shapes with their mouth when speaking. For example, English has one *k* sound while Russian uses two *k* sounds to give different meanings, and the English *r* and *l* sounds do not exist in Japanese!

Animal sounds

Dogs, cats, and some other animals make sounds from their throats, rather like we do. Other animals use different body parts to make sounds. The beaver slaps its tail against water to scare off enemies. Male tree-frogs tap **hollow** trees to make sounds to call other frogs. A hummingbird hums by quickly beating its wings – up to 70 times a second!

Male crickets make sounds by rubbing a scraper on one front wing along a row of bumps on the other.

Lyrebird

Amazing lyrebirds in Australia can copy lots of other sounds. These 1-metre (3-foot) long birds mimic other bird calls, and sounds of machines such as car alarms and chainsaws!

Activity: Make cricket sounds

Make sounds like a cricket does!

What you need
- Long-sleeved top
- Two sheets of sandpaper
- Two large elastic bands

What to do

1 Wear a long-sleeved top and ask someone to help you wrap a piece of sandpaper around one arm. Fix it in place with an elastic band.

2 Do the same on the other arm.

3 Now, fold your arms and rub the two pieces of sandpaper together to make sounds. This is what happens when a cricket rubs its wings together.

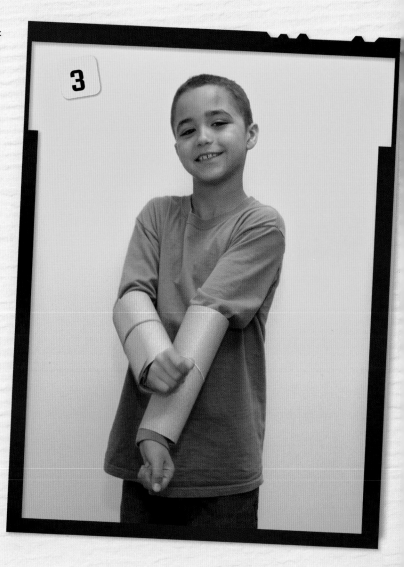

3

Glossary

hollow something that has a hole or empty space inside it

larynx area at the top of the throat that contains the vocal cords

lung body part found in the chest that is used for breathing

mallet hammer with a large wooden head

material something we use or make other things from, such as wood, rubber, or plastic

membrane very thin layer of material, such as skin or plastic

mouthpiece part of a musical instrument that you put to your lips

muscle type of body part that can pull on other body parts to make them move

percussion type of musical instrument that you play by hitting it

pick small piece of metal or plastic that you use to pluck strings on a guitar

reed thin piece of wood in the mouthpiece of a musical instrument that vibrates quickly and makes a sound when you blow air across it

sound wave vibration in the air that we hear as sound

trachea tube in the neck and chest that carries air to and from the lungs

vibrate, vibration move forwards and backwards or up and down very quickly, again and again

vocal cords body parts that are stretched across the larynx in the throat. They vibrate when air goes past them to make the sound of our voice.

Find out more

Books

A Cry in the Dark: Sound and the Science of Survival (Science Adventures), Richard and Louise Spilsbury (Franklin Watts, 2014)

Light and Sound (Super Science Experiments), Chris Oxlade (Miles Kelly Publishing Ltd, 2011)

Musical Instruments (Make and Use), Anna-Marie D'Cruz (Wayland, 2010)

Sound (The Science Detective Investigates), Harriet McGregor (Wayland, 2011)

Websites

www.bbc.co.uk/learningzone/clips/understanding-sound-and-vibrations/1604.html

www.bbc.co.uk/learningzone/clips/sound-and-vibration/6.html

www.bbc.co.uk/learningzone/clips/sounds-made-by-musical-instruments/2417.html

Watch these clips to see how sound is made by vibrations and how different instruments make sound.

www.kidshealth.org/kid/ill_injure/sick/laryngitis.html

You can find out more about how the voice works and why it sometimes does not work on this website.

www.sciencekids.co.nz/sound.html

There are facts, quizzes, and experiments about making sound on this website.

www.seaworld.org/animal-info/sound-library

You can listen to some of the sounds different animals make on this website.

Index